PASTA FOR DINNER

AN EASY PASTA COOKBOOK WITH DELICIOUS PASTA RECIPES

By
BookSumo Press
Copyright © by Saxonberg Associates

Published by
BookSumo Press, a DBA of Saxonberg Associates
http://www.booksumo.com/

ABOUT THE AUTHOR.

BookSumo Press is a publisher of unique, easy, and healthy cookbooks.

Our cookbooks span all topics and all subjects. If you want a deep dive into the possibilities of cooking with any type of ingredient. Then BookSumo Press is your go to place for robust yet simple and delicious cookbooks and recipes. Whether you are looking for great tasting pressure cooker recipes or authentic ethic and cultural food. BookSumo Press has a delicious and easy cookbook for you.

With simple ingredients, and even simpler step-by-step instructions BookSumo cookbooks get everyone in the kitchen chefing delicious meals.

BookSumo is an independent publisher of books operating in the beautiful Garden State (NJ) and our team of chefs and kitchen experts are here to teach, eat, and be merry!

INTRODUCTION

Welcome to *The Effortless Chef Series*! Thank you for taking the time to purchase this cookbook.

Come take a journey into the delights of easy cooking. The point of this cookbook and all BookSumo Press cookbooks is to exemplify the effortless nature of cooking simply.

In this book we focus on Pasta. You will find that even though the recipes are simple, the taste of the dishes are quite amazing.

So will you take an adventure in simple cooking? If the answer is yes please consult the table of contents to find the dishes you are most interested in.

Once you are ready, jump right in and start cooking.

— BookSumo Press

TABLE OF CONTENTS

Any Issues? Contact Us

If you find that something important to you is missing from this book please contact us at info@booksumo.com.

We will take your concerns into consideration when the 2nd edition of this book is published. And we will keep you updated!

— BookSumo Press

LEGAL NOTES

COMMON ABBREVIATIONS

cup(s)	C.
tablespoon	tbsp
teaspoon	tsp
ounce	oz.
pound	lb

*All units used are standard American measurements

CHAPTER 1: EASY PASTA RECIPES

ROSEMARY PASTA SHELLS SOUP

Ingredients

- 2 tsps olive oil
- 1 garlic clove, finely minced
- 1 shallot, finely diced
- 3 -4 C. fat free chicken broth or 3 -4 C. vegetable stock
- 1 (14 1/2 oz) can diced tomatoes
- 1 (14 1/2 oz) can white beans (cannellini or other)
- 1/2 C. whole wheat pasta shells or 1/2 C. shell pasta
- 1 tsp rosemary
- 3 C. Baby Spinach, cleaned and trimmed
- 1/8 tsp black pepper
- 1 dash crushed red pepper flakes

Directions

- Place a large saucepan on medium heat. Heat the oil in it. Add the garlic and shallot then cook them for 4 min.
- Stir in the broth, tomatoes, beans and rosemary, black and red pepper. Cook them until they start boiling. Stir in the pasta and simmer the soup for 12 min.

- Stir in the spinach and simmer the soup until it wilts. Serve the soup warm.
- Enjoy.

Servings Per Recipe: 4

Timing Information:

Total Time	25mins
Prep Time	8 mins
Cook Time	17 mins

Nutritional Information:

Calories	218.4
Fat	3.3 g
Cholesterol	0 mg
Sodium	726.3 mg
Carbohydrates	37.9 g
Protein	12 g

* Percent Daily Values are based on a 2,000 calorie diet.

BELL PASTA SOUP

Ingredients

- 1 tbsp olive oil
- 1 onion, chopped
- 2 cloves garlic, minced
- 1 red bell pepper, chopped
- 3 C. low fat, low chicken broth
- 1 C. canned whole tomatoes, chopped
- 1 1/2 C. kidney beans, cooked
- 2 tsps chopped fresh thyme
- 1/2 C. chopped spinach
- 1 C. seashell pasta
- ground black pepper to taste

Directions

- Place a large pot on medium heat. Heat the oil in it. Add the onion and garlic then cook them for 5 min. Stir in the bell pepper and cook them for 3 min.
- Stir in the broth, tomatoes and beans. Cook them until they start boiling. Lower the heat and simmer the soup for 20 min.
- Add the thyme, spinach and pasta. Cook the soup for 5 min. Adjust the seasoning of the soup. Serve it warm.

- Enjoy.

Servings Per Recipe: 8

Timing Information:

Preparation	10 m
Cooking	20 m
Total Time	40 m

Nutritional Information:

Calories	174 kcal
Fat	3.1 g
Carbohydrates	29g
Protein	8 g
Cholesterol	0 mg
Sodium	409 mg

* Percent Daily Values are based on a 2,000 calorie diet.

SMOKED SUNDRIED TOMATO SOUP

Ingredients

- 2 slices turkey bacon, finely chopped
- 1 onion, chopped
- 1 clove garlic, minced
- 1/4 tsp freshly grated nutmeg (optional)
- 1/8 tsp crushed red pepper flakes (optional)
- 6 C. chicken broth, or more as needed
- 1 (15 oz) can cannellini beans, drained and rinsed - or more to taste
- 2 tbsps chopped sun-dried tomatoes
- 2 oz Parmesan cheese rind
- 1 bunch red or white Swiss chard
- 1/4 C. uncooked small pasta, such as orzo or pastina
- 5 large fresh sage leaves, minced
- 5 leaves fresh basil, coarsely chopped (optional)
- 1 tbsp grated Parmesan cheese, divided (optional)
- 1 tbsp extra-virgin olive oil, divided (optional)

Directions

- Place a large saucepan on medium heat. Add the bacon, onion, garlic, nutmeg, and red pepper flakes then cook them for 5 min.

- Stir in the chicken broth and cannellini beans then cook them until they start boiling. Add the sun-dried tomatoes and the piece of Parmesan cheese rind.
- Cook the soup on low heat for 10 min.
- Slice the stems of the chard into 3/4 inch ling and the leaves into 1 inch wide slices. Add the stems with pasta to the soup then cook them for 10 min on low heat.
- Add the sliced chard leaves, sage, and basil then cook it for 5 min on low heat. Serve the soup warm with cheese.
- Enjoy.

Servings Per Recipe: 8

Timing Information:

Preparation	25 m
Cooking	30 m
Total Time	55 m

Nutritional Information:

Calories	215 kcal
Fat	9.7 g
Carbohydrates	22.2g
Protein	9.9 g
Cholesterol	14 mg
Sodium	494 mg

* Percent Daily Values are based on a 2,000 calorie diet.

CRIMINI PASTA BAKE

INGREDIENTS

- 8 h crimini mushrooms
- 1 C. broccoli floret
- 1 C. spinach, fresh leaf, tightly packed
- 2 red bell peppers, julienned
- 1 large onion, chopped
- 1 C. mozzarella cheese, shredded
- 1 C. tomato sauce
- 2/3 lb pasta (fettuccine or penne works well)
- 1/3 C. parmesan cheese, grated
- 3 tbsps herbes de provence
- 2 tbsps extra virgin olive oil
- 1 tbsp salt
- 1/2 tbsp pepper

DIRECTIONS

- Before you do anything set the oven to 450 F. Grease a casserole dish with oil or cooking spray.
- Get a large mixing bowl: Toss the mushrooms, broccoli, spinach, pepper, and onion in it. Add 1 tbsp of olive oil, salt, pepper and toss them again.

- Spread the veggies in the greased dish and cook it in the oven for 10 min.
- Cook the pasta until it becomes dente. Drain the pasta and set it aside.
- Get a large mixing bowl: Mix 1 tbsp of olive oil with baked veggies, pasta, herbs and mozzarella cheese. Spread the mix back in the casserole dish.
- Sprinkle the cheese on top then cook it for 20 min. Serve it warm and enjoy.

Servings Per Recipe: 6

Timing Information:

Total Time	50mins
Prep Time	15 mins
Cook Time	35 MINS

Nutritional Information:

Calories	354.1
Fat	11.4 g
Cholesterol	19.6 mg
Sodium	1593.8 mg
Carbohydrates	48.2 g
Protein	15.6 g

* Percent Daily Values are based on a 2,000 calorie diet.

ROMANO RIGATONI CASSEROLE

INGREDIENTS

- 1 lb ground sausage (I use Sage flavor)
- 1 (28 oz) can Italian-style tomato sauce
- 1 (14 1/2 oz) can cannellini beans, drained and rinsed
- 1 (16 oz) BOX rigatoni pasta
- ½ tsp minced garlic
- 1 tsp italian seasoning
- 3 C. shredded mozzarella cheese
- ¼ C. romano cheese, grated
- chopped parsley, to garnish

DIRECTIONS

- Before you do anything set the oven to 350 F. Grease a large casserole dish with some butter or oil.
- Place a large pot on medium heat. Add the garlic with sausages and cook them for 6 min. Add the tomato sauce, beans and Italian seasoning then cook them for 5 min on low heat.
- Cook the pasta according to the manufacturer's directions. Drain the pasta and sit it into the pot.

- Pour half of the sausage pasta mix in the greased casserole then top it with half of the mozzarella cheese. Repeat the process to make another layer.
- Top the casserole with romano cheese then put on it a piece of foil. Cook the rigatoni casserole in the oven for 26 min.
- Serve your rigatoni warm.
- Enjoy.

Servings Per Recipe: 6

Timing Information:

Total Time	55mins
Prep Time	30 mins
Cook Time	25 MINS

Nutritional Information:

Calories	795.6
Fat	37.6 g
Cholesterol	166.2 mg
Sodium	1842.2 mg
Carbohydrates	73.2 g
Protein	41.2 g

* Percent Daily Values are based on a 2,000 calorie diet.

CHEESY CHICKEN CREAM PASTA

INGREDIENTS

- 1 1⁄2 C. flour, plus
- 1 tbsp flour
- 1 tbsp salt
- 2 tsps black pepper
- 2 tsps Italian herb seasoning
- 3 lbs boneless skinless chicken breasts
- 3 fluid oz vegetable oil, divided
- 1 lb penne pasta
- 1 tbsp garlic, chopped
- 1 red pepper, julienne cut
- 1⁄2 C. white wine
- 1⁄2 lb whole spinach leaves, stemmed
- 12 fluid oz heavy cream
- 1 C. parmesan cheese, grated

DIRECTIONS

- Before you do anything set the oven to 350 F.
- Get a shallow dish: Mix in it 1 1/2 C. flour, salt, black pepper and Italian herb seasoning. Place a large oven proof skillet on medium heat then heat in it some oil.

- Coat the chicken breasts with the flour mix then brown it in the skillet for 4 min on each side. Transfer the skillet with chicken to the oven and cook it for 17 min.
- Cook the penne pasta by following the directions on the package until it becomes dente. Drain it and place it aside.
- To make the sauce:
- Place a large saucepan on medium heat. Add to it 1 oz of oil. Cook in it the red pepper with garlic for 1 min. Stir in the flour.
- Stir in the wine and coo them for 1 min. Add the cream and spinach then cook them until they start boiling. Stir in the cheese until it melts.
- Get a large mixing bowl: Toss the pasta with 1/2 of the sauce. Serve the pasta warm with chicken then drizzle the remaining sauce on top.
- Enjoy.

Servings Per Recipe: 6

Timing Information:

Total Time	1hr
Prep Time	45 mins
Cook Time	15 MINS

Nutritional Information:

Calories	1081.4
Fat	48.5 g
Cholesterol	241.6 mg
Sodium	1738.5 mg
Carbohydrates	91.5 g
Protein	66.3 g

* Percent Daily Values are based on a 2,000 calorie diet.

Sunny Hot Spaghetti

INGREDIENTS

- 2 1/2 C. cooked spaghetti
- 1/4 C. olive oil
- 8 pepperoncini peppers, finely minced
- 1/2 C. spaghetti sauce (Muir Glen Garlic Roasted Garlic is by far the best I've found)
- 1 tsp oregano
- 1 tsp garlic granules or 2 tbsps fresh garlic, minced fine

DIRECTIONS

- Place a large pan on medium heat. Heat the oil in it. Add the herbs with peppers and cook them for 4 min.
- Stir in the sauce with cooked spaghetti then cook it for 3 min.
- Serve your spaghetti warm right away.
- Enjoy.

Servings Per Recipe: 2

Timing Information:

Total Time	16mins
Prep Time	4 mins
Cook Time	12 MINS

Nutritional Information:

Calories	627.9
Fat	30.4 g
Cholesterol	0 mg
Sodium	3728.5 mg
Carbohydrates	77.1 g
Protein	14.2 g

* Percent Daily Values are based on a 2,000 calorie diet.

SAUCY BEEF SKILLET

INGREDIENTS

- 500 g minced beef
- 4 tbsps olive oil
- 1 onion, finely diced
- 2 garlic cloves, peeled and crushed
- 1 tsp allspice
- 1 tsp cinnamon
- 1 tsp paprika
- 130 g tomato paste
- 500 g pasta sauce
- 1 tbsp beef stock, dried instant
- 2 bay leaves
- Worcestershire sauce, dash

DIRECTION

- Place a large pan on high heat. Heat the oil in it. Add the onion, garlic, beef and spices then cook them for 6 min.
- Stir in the tomato and pasta sauce, paprika, beef stock, bay leaves, salt and pepper then cook them for 30 min on low heat while stirring often.
- Serve your saucy beef warm with some pasta.
- Enjoy.

Servings Per Recipe: 6

Timing Information:

Total Time	45mins
Prep Time	5 mins
Cook Time	40 MINS

Nutritional Information:

Calories	361.1
Fat	24 g
Cholesterol	58.3 mg
Sodium	578.8 mg
Carbohydrates	18.4 g
Protein	18.3 g

* Percent Daily Values are based on a 2,000 calorie diet

PUTTANESCA

(SOUTHERN ITALIAN STYLE)

Ingredients

- 8 oz. pasta
- 1/2 C. olive oil
- 3 cloves garlic, minced
- 2 C. diced tomatoes, pushed through a sieve
- 4 anchovy filets, rinsed and diced
- 2 tbsps tomato paste
- 3 tbsps capers
- 20 Greek olives, pitted and coarsely diced
- 1/2 tsp crushed red pepper flakes

Directions

- Boil your pasta in water and salt for 9 mins then remove all the liquids.
- Now being to stir fry your garlic in oil until it is browned all over.
- Then add the tomatoes and cook the mix for 7 mins before adding in: the pepper flakes, anchovies, olives, tomato paste, and capers.

- Let the mix cook for 12 mins and stir everything at least 2 times.
- Now add in the pasta and stir everything to evenly coat the noodles.
- Enjoy.

Amount per serving (4 total)

Timing Information:

Preparation	25 m
Cooking	15 m
Total Time	40 m

Nutritional Information:

Calories	490 kcal
Fat	34 g
Carbohydrates	38.7g
Protein	9.3 g
Cholesterol	44 mg
Sodium	728 mg

* Percent Daily Values are based on a 2,000 calorie diet.

CLASSICAL PENNE PASTA

Ingredients

- 1 (16 oz.) package penne pasta
- 2 tbsps olive oil
- 1/4 C. diced red onion
- 1 tbsp diced garlic
- 1/4 C. white wine
- 2 (14.5 oz.) cans diced tomatoes
- 1 lb shrimp, peeled and deveined
- 1 C. grated Parmesan cheese

Directions

- Boil your pasta in water and salt for 9 mins then remove the liquids.
- Now begin to stir fry your garlic and onions in oil until the onions are soft.
- Then add in the tomatoes and wine.
- Simmer the mix for 12 mins while stirring. Then add in the shrimp and cook everything for 6 mins.

- Now add the pasta and stir everything to evenly coat the noodles.
- Enjoy.

Amount per serving (8 total)

Timing Information:

Preparation	10 m
Cooking	25 m
Total Time	35 m

Nutritional Information:

Calories	385 kcal
Fat	8.5 g
Carbohydrates	48.5g
Protein	24.5 g
Cholesterol	95 mg
Sodium	399 mg

* Percent Daily Values are based on a 2,000 calorie diet.

PARMESAN ORZO

Ingredients

- 1/2 C. butter, divided
- 8 pearl onions
- 1 C. uncooked orzo pasta
- 1/2 C. sliced fresh mushrooms
- 1 C. water
- 1/2 C. white wine
- garlic powder to taste
- salt and pepper to taste
- 1/2 C. grated Parmesan cheese
- 1/4 C. fresh parsley

Directions

- Stir fry your onions in half of the butter until it is browned then add in the rest of the butter, mushrooms, and the orzo.
- Continue frying everything for 7 mins.
- Now combine in the wine and the water and get everything boiling.

- Once the mix is boiling, set the heat to low, and cook everything for 9 mins after adding in the pepper, salt and garlic powder.
- Once the orzo is done top it with parsley and parmesan.
- Enjoy.

Amount per serving (6 total)

Timing Information:

Preparation	15 m
Cooking	25 m
Total Time	40 m

Nutritional Information:

Calories	327 kcal
Fat	18.6 g
Carbohydrates	28.1g
Protein	8.6 g
Cholesterol	48 mg
Sodium	306 mg

* Percent Daily Values are based on a 2,000 calorie diet.

PASTA RUSTICA

Ingredients

- 1 lb farfalle (bow tie) pasta
- 1/3 C. olive oil
- 1 clove garlic, chopped
- 1/4 C. butter
- 2 small zucchini, quartered and sliced
- 1 onion, chopped
- 1 tomato, chopped
- 1 (8 oz) package mushrooms, sliced
- 1 tbsp dried oregano
- 1 tbsp paprika
- salt and pepper to taste

Directions

- Boil your pasta for 10 mins in water and salt. Remove excess liquid and set aside.
- Fry your salt, pepper, garlic, paprika, zucchini, oregano, mushrooms, onion, and tomato, for 17 mins in olive oil.
- Mix the veggies and pasta.
- Enjoy.

Servings: 4 servings

Timing Information:

Preparation	Cooking	Total Time
10 mins	25 mins	35 mins

Nutritional Information:

Calories	717 kcal
Carbohydrates	92.8 g
Cholesterol	31 mg
Fat	32.9 g
Fiber	7.5 g
Protein	18.1 g
Sodium	491 mg

* Percent Daily Values are based on a 2,000 calorie diet.

CLASSICAL ALFREDO

Ingredients

- 6 skinless, boneless chicken breast halves - cut into cubes
- 6 tbsps butter, divided
- 4 cloves garlic, minced, divided
- 1 tbsp Italian seasoning
- 1 lb fettuccini pasta
- 1 onion, diced
- 1 (8 oz.) package sliced mushrooms
- 1/3 C. all-purpose flour
- 1 tbsp salt
- 3/4 tsp ground white pepper
- 3 C. milk
- 1 C. half-and-half
- 3/4 C. grated Parmesan cheese
- 8 oz. shredded Colby-Monterey Jack cheese
- 3 roma (plum) tomatoes, diced
- 1/2 C. sour cream

Directions

- Stir your chicken after coating it with Italian seasoning in 2 tbsp of butter with 2 pieces of garlic.

- Stir fry the meat until it is fully done then place everything to the side.
- Now boil your pasta in water and salt for 9 mins then remove all the liquids.
- At the same time stir fry your onions in 4 tbsp of butter along with the mushrooms and 2 more pieces of garlic.
- Continue frying the mix until the onions are see-through then combine in your pepper, salt, and flour.
- Stir and cook the mix for 4 mins. Then gradually add in your half and half and the milk, while stirring, until everything is smooth.
- Combine in the Monterey and parmesan and let the mix cook until the cheese has melted then add the chicken, sour cream, and tomatoes.
- Serve your pasta topped liberally with the chicken mix and sauce.
- Enjoy.

Amount per serving (8 total)

Timing Information:

Preparation	30 m
Cooking	30 m
Total Time	1 h

Nutritional Information:

Calories	673 kcal
Fat	30.8 g
Carbohydrates	57g
Protein	43.3 g
Cholesterol	133 mg
Sodium	1386 mg

* Percent Daily Values are based on a 2,000 calorie diet.

EASY ITALIAN PARMIGIANA

Ingredients

- 1 egg, beaten
- 2 oz. dry bread crumbs
- 2 skinless, boneless chicken breast halves
- 3/4 (16 oz.) jar spaghetti sauce
- 2 oz. shredded mozzarella cheese
- 1/4 C. grated Parmesan cheese

Directions

- Coat a cookie sheet with oil then set your oven to 350 degrees before doing anything else.
- Get a bowl and add in your eggs.
- Get a 2nd bowl and add in your bread crumbs.
- Coat your chicken first with the eggs then with the bread crumbs.
- Lay your pieces of chicken on the cookie sheet and cook them in the oven for 45 mins, until they are fully done.
- Now add half of your pasta sauce to a casserole dish and lay in your chicken on top of the sauce.

- Place the rest of the sauce on top of the chicken pieces. Then add a topping of parmesan and mozzarella over everything.
- Cook the parmigiana in the oven for 25 mins.
- Enjoy.

Amount per serving (2 total)

Timing Information:

Preparation	30 m
Cooking	1 h
Total Time	1 h 30 m

Nutritional Information:

Calories	528 kcal
Fat	18.3 g
Carbohydrates	44.9g
Protein	43.5 g
Cholesterol	184 mg
Sodium	1309 mg

* Percent Daily Values are based on a 2,000 calorie diet.

Maggie's Favorite Pasta

Ingredients

- 2 tbsps olive oil
- 1 anchovy fillet
- 2 tbsps capers
- 3 cloves minced garlic
- 1/2 C. dry white wine
- 1/4 tsp dried oregano
- 1 pinch red pepper flakes, or to taste
- 3 C. crushed Italian (plum) tomatoes
- salt and ground black pepper to taste
- 1 pinch cayenne pepper, or to taste
- 1 (7 oz.) can oil-packed tuna, drained
- 1/4 C. diced fresh flat-leaf parsley
- 1 (12 oz.) package spaghetti
- 1 tbsp extra-virgin olive oil, or to taste
- 1/4 C. freshly grated Parmigiano-Reggiano cheese, or to taste
- 1 tbsp diced fresh flat-leaf parsley, or to taste

Directions

- Stir fry your capers and anchovies in olive oil for 4 mins then combine in the garlic and continue frying the mix for 2 more mins.
- Now add: pepper flakes, white wine, and orange.
- Stir the mix and turn up the heat.
- Let the mix cook for 5 mins before adding the tomatoes and getting the mix to a gentle simmer.
- Once the mix is simmering add in: cayenne, black pepper, and salt.
- Set the heat to low and let everything cook for 12 mins.
- Now begin to boil your pasta in water and salt for 10 mins then remove all the liquids and leave the noodles in the pan.
- Combine the simmering tomatoes with the noodles and place a lid on the pot. With a low level of heat warm everything for 4 mins.
- When serving your pasta top it with some Parmigiano-Reggiano, parsley, and olive oil.
- Enjoy.

Amount per serving (4 total)

Timing Information:

Preparation	20 m
Cooking	35 m
Total Time	55 m

Nutritional Information:

Calories	619 kcal
Fat	17.7 g
Carbohydrates	79.5g
Protein	31.2 g
Cholesterol	14 mg
Sodium	706 mg

* Percent Daily Values are based on a 2,000 calorie diet.

CHICKEN FROM MILAN

Ingredients

- 1 tbsp butter
- 2 cloves garlic, minced
- 1/2 C. sun-dried tomatoes, diced
- 1 C. chicken broth, divided
- 1 C. heavy cream
- 1 lb skinless, boneless chicken breast halves
- salt and pepper to taste
- 2 tbsps vegetable oil
- 2 tbsps diced fresh basil
- 8 oz. dry fettuccini pasta

Directions

- Stir fry your garlic for 1 min, in butter, then combine in 3/4 C. of broth and the tomatoes.
- Turn up the heat and get everything boiling.
- Once the mix is boiling, set the heat to low, and let the contents cook for 12 mins.
- Now add in the cream and get everything boiling again until the mix is thick.

- Coat your chicken all over with pepper and salt then fry the meat in hot oil for 5 mins each side until fully done. Then place the chicken to the side in a covered bowl.
- Remove some of the drippings from the pan and begin to get 1/4 C. of broth boiling while scraping the bottom bits.
- Once the mix is boiling, set the heat to low, add in the basil, and let the broth reduce a bit.
- Once it has reduced, combine it with the tomato cream sauce.
- Now begin to boil your pasta in water and salt for 9 mins then remove the liquid and place everything in a bowl.
- Stir the pasta with about 5 tbsps of tomato cream sauce.
- Now slice your chicken into strips and get the tomato hot again.
- Divide your noodles between serving dishes.
- Top the noodles with some chicken and then some sauce.
- Enjoy.

Amount per serving (4 total)

Timing Information:

Preparation	10 m
Cooking	20 m
Total Time	30 m

Nutritional Information:

Calories	641 kcal
Fat	34.8 g
Carbohydrates	47g
Protein	36.3 g
Cholesterol	156 mg
Sodium	501 mg

* Percent Daily Values are based on a 2,000 calorie diet.

CLASSICAL LASAGNA I

Ingredients

- 1 1/2 lbs lean ground beef
- 1 onion, diced
- 2 cloves garlic, minced
- 1 tbsp diced fresh basil
- 1 tsp dried oregano
- 2 tbsps brown sugar
- 1 1/2 tsps salt
- 1 (29 oz.) can diced tomatoes
- 2 (6 oz.) cans tomato paste
- 12 dry lasagna noodles
- 2 eggs, beaten
- 1 pint part-skim ricotta cheese
- 1/2 C. grated Parmesan cheese
- 2 tbsps dried parsley
- 1 tsp salt
- 1 lb mozzarella cheese, shredded
- 2 tbsps grated Parmesan cheese

Directions

- Stir fry your garlic, onions, and beef for 3 mins then combine in: tomato paste, basil, diced tomatoes, oregano, 1.5 tsp salt, and brown sugar.
- Now set your oven to 375 degrees before doing anything else.
- Begin to boil your pasta in water and salt for 9 mins then remove all the liquids.
- Get a bowl, combine: 1 tsp salt, eggs, parsley, ricotta, and parmesan.
- Place a third of the pasta in a casserole dish and top everything with half of the cheese mix, one third of the sauce, and 1/2 of the mozzarella.
- Continue layering in this manner until all the ingredients have been used up.
- Then top everything with some more parmesan.
- Cook the lasagna in the oven for 35 mins.
- Enjoy.

Amount per serving (8 total)

Timing Information:

Preparation	30 m
Cooking	1 h 30 m
Total Time	2 h

Nutritional Information:

Calories	664 kcal
Fat	29.5 g
Carbohydrates	48.3g
Protein	50.9 g
Cholesterol	1168 mg
Sodium	1900 mg

* Percent Daily Values are based on a 2,000 calorie diet.

Classical Lasagna II

Ingredients

- 1 lb sweet Italian sausage
- 3/4 lb lean ground beef
- 1/2 C. minced onion
- 2 cloves garlic, crushed
- 1 (28 oz.) can crushed tomatoes
- 2 (6 oz.) cans tomato paste
- 2 (6.5 oz.) cans canned tomato sauce
- 1/2 C. water
- 2 tbsps white sugar
- 1 1/2 tsps dried basil leaves
- 1/2 tsp fennel seeds
- 1 tsp Italian seasoning
- 1 tbsp salt
- 1/4 tsp ground black pepper
- 4 tbsps diced fresh parsley
- 12 lasagna noodles
- 16 oz. ricotta cheese
- 1 egg
- 1/2 tsp salt
- 3/4 lb mozzarella cheese, sliced
- 3/4 C. grated Parmesan cheese

Directions

- Stir fry your garlic, sausage, onion, and beef until the meat is fully done. Then add in: 2 tbsp parsley, crushed tomatoes, pepper, tomato paste, 1 tbsp salt, tomato sauce, Italian spice, water, fennel seeds, sugar, and basil.
- Get the mix boiling, set the heat to low, and let the contents gently cook for 90 mins. Stir the mix at least 4 times.
- Now get your pasta boiling in water and salt for 9 mins then remove the liquids.
- Get a bowl, combine: 1/2 tsp salt, ricotta, the rest of the parsley, and the eggs.
- Set your oven to 375 degrees before doing anything else.
- Coat the bottom of a casserole dish with 1.5 C. of the meat and tomato mix then place six pieces of lasagna on top.
- Add half of the cheese mix then 1/3 of the mozzarella.
- Add 1.5 C. of tomato meat mix again and a quarter of a C. of parmesan.
- Continue layering in this manner until all the ingredients have been used up.
- Try to end with mozzarella and parmesan.
- Take a large piece of foil and coat it with nonstick spray then cover the casserole dish with the foil and cook everything in the oven for 30 mins.

- Now take off the foil and continue cooking the lasagna for 20 more mins.
- Serve the dish after letting everything rest for at least 30 mins (longer is better).
- Enjoy.

Amount per serving (12 total)

Timing Information:

Preparation	30 m
Cooking	2 h 30 m
Total Time	3 h 15 m

Nutritional Information:

Calories	448 kcal
Fat	21.3 g
Carbohydrates	36.5g
Protein	29.7 g
Cholesterol	82 mg
Sodium	1788 mg

* Percent Daily Values are based on a 2,000 calorie diet.

ROMAN FUN PASTA

Ingredients

- 1 (12 oz.) package bow tie pasta
- 2 tbsps olive oil
- 1 lb sweet Italian sausage, casings removed and crumbled
- 1/2 tsp red pepper flakes
- 1/2 C. diced onion
- 3 cloves garlic, minced
- 1 (28 oz.) can Italian-style plum tomatoes, drained and coarsely diced
- 1 1/2 C. heavy cream
- 1/2 tsp salt
- 3 tbsps minced fresh parsley

Directions

- Boil your pasta in water and salt for 9 mins then remove the liquids.
- Begin to stir fry your pepper flakes and sausage in oil until it the meat is browned then add the garlic and onions.
- Let the onions cook until they are soft then add in the salt, cream, and tomatoes.
- Stir the mix then get everything gently boiling.

- Let the mix gently cook with a low level of heat for 9 mins then add in the pasta.
- Stir the mix, to evenly cook the noodles, then coat everything with parsley.
- Enjoy.

Amount per serving (6 total)

Timing Information:

Preparation	15 m
Cooking	30 m
Total Time	45 m

Nutritional Information:

Calories	656 kcal
Fat	42.1 g
Carbohydrates	50.9g
Protein	20.1 g
Cholesterol	111 mg
Sodium	1088 mg

* Percent Daily Values are based on a 2,000 calorie diet.

Tortellini Classico

Ingredients

- 1 lb sweet Italian sausage, casings removed
- 1 C. diced onion
- 2 cloves garlic, minced
- 5 C. beef broth
- 1/2 C. water
- 1/2 C. red wine
- 4 large tomatoes - peeled, seeded and diced
- 1 C. thinly sliced carrots
- 1/2 tbsp packed fresh basil leaves
- 1/2 tsp dried oregano
- 1 (8 oz.) can tomato sauce
- 1 1/2 C. sliced zucchini
- 8 oz. fresh tortellini pasta
- 3 tbsps diced fresh parsley

Directions

- In a large pot brown your sausage all over.
- Then remove the meat from the pan.

- Begin to stir fry your garlic and onions in the drippings then add in: the sausage, broth, tomato sauce, water, oregano, wine, basil, tomatoes, and carrots.
- Get the mix boiling, set the heat to low, and let everything cook for 35 mins.
- Remove any fat which rises to the top then add in the parsley and zucchini.
- Continue cooking the mix for 20 more mins before adding in the pasta and letting everything cooking 15 more mins.
- When serving the dish top it with parmesan.
- Enjoy.

Amount per serving (8 total)

Timing Information:

Preparation	20 m
Cooking	1 h 15 m
Total Time	1 h 35 m

Nutritional Information:

Calories	324 kcal
Fat	20.2 g
Carbohydrates	19.1g
Protein	14.6 g
Cholesterol	50 mg
Sodium	1145 mg

* Percent Daily Values are based on a 2,000 calorie diet.

Feta Fettucine

Ingredients

- 1 bunch diced fresh cilantro
- 6 tbsps pine nuts
- 1 tsp lemon juice, or to taste
- 1/3 C. crumbled feta cheese
- salt and ground black pepper to taste
- 1/2 C. olive oil
- 1 (12 oz.) package fettucine pasta
- 1 tsp extra-virgin olive oil

Directions

- Pulse the following in a food processor until minced: black pepper, cilantro, salt, pine nuts, feta cheese, and lemon juice.
- Now slowly add in half a C. of olive oil while continually running the processor.
- Boil your pasta for 9 mins in water and salt then remove the liquids.
- Place the pasta in a bowl and top it with the cilantro sauce.

- Toss the mix then add some olive oil and toss everything again.
- Enjoy.

Amount per serving (4 total)

Timing Information:

Preparation	15 m
Cooking	10 m
Total Time	25 m

Nutritional Information:

Calories	663 kcal
Fat	39.4 g
Carbohydrates	64.8g
Protein	16.5 g
Cholesterol	11 mg
Sodium	248 mg

* Percent Daily Values are based on a 2,000 calorie diet.

TORTELLINI

Ingredients

- 1 (16 oz.) package cheese tortellini
- 1 (14.5 oz.) can diced tomatoes with garlic and onion
- 1 C. diced fresh spinach
- 1/2 tsp salt
- 1/4 tsp pepper
- 1 1/2 tsps dried basil
- 1 tsp minced garlic
- 2 tbsps all-purpose flour
- 3/4 C. milk
- 3/4 C. heavy cream
- 1/4 C. grated Parmesan cheese

Directions

- Boil your pasta in water and salt for 9 mins then remove the liquids.
- At the same time heat and stir the following in a large pot: garlic, tomatoes, basil, spinach, pepper and salt.
- Once the mix begins to simmer add in a mix of cream, milk, and flour.

- Stir the mix until everything is smooth then add the parmesan and set the heat to low.
- Let the mix gently boil for 4 mins then add in your pasta to the sauce after it has cooked.
- Stir everything.
- Enjoy.

Amount per serving (6 total)

Timing Information:

Preparation	20 m
Cooking	20 m
Total Time	40 m

Nutritional Information:

Calories	400 kcal
Fat	19.7 g
Carbohydrates	43.9g
Protein	14.8 g
Cholesterol	79 mg
Sodium	885 mg

* Percent Daily Values are based on a 2,000 calorie diet.

Restaurant Style Primavera

Ingredients

- 1 (16 oz.) package uncooked farfalle pasta
- 1 lb hot Italian turkey sausage, cut into 1/2 inch slices
- 1/2 C. olive oil, divided
- 4 cloves garlic, diced
- 1/2 onion, diced
- 2 small zucchini, diced
- 2 small yellow squash, diced
- 6 roma (plum) tomatoes, diced
- 1 green bell pepper, diced
- 20 leaves fresh basil
- 2 tsps chicken bouillon granules
- 1/2 tsp red pepper flakes
- 1/2 C. grated Parmesan cheese

Directions

- Cook your pasta in water and salt for 9 mins then remove all the liquids.
- Stir fry your sausage until fully done then remove it from the pan.

- Now begin to stir fry your onions and garlic until the mix is hot then add in: basil, zucchini, bell peppers, squash, and tomatoes.
- Stir the mix then add in the bouillon and evenly mix it in.
- Once the bouillon has been added.
- Combine in the red pepper and the rest of the oil.
- Keep cooking the mix for 12 more mins then stir in the cheese, sausage, and pasta.
- Let everything get hot for 7 mins.
- Enjoy.

Amount per serving (8 total)

Timing Information:

Preparation	20 m
Cooking	30 m
Total Time	50 m

Nutritional Information:

Calories	477 kcal
Fat	21.8 g
Carbohydrates	50.1g
Protein	20.5 g
Cholesterol	38 mg
Sodium	621 mg

* Percent Daily Values are based on a 2,000 calorie diet.

AUTHENTIC ITALIAN TETRAZZINI

Ingredients

- 2 (8 oz.) packages angel hair pasta
- 1/4 C. butter
- 2/3 C. sliced onion
- 1/4 C. all-purpose flour
- 2 C. milk
- 1 tsp salt
- 1/4 tsp ground white pepper
- 1/2 tsp poultry seasoning
- 1/4 tsp ground mustard
- 1 C. shredded sharp Cheddar cheese, divided
- 2 tbsps diced pimento peppers (optional)
- 1 (4.5 oz.) can sliced mushrooms
- 1 lb cooked turkey, sliced

Directions

- Set your oven to 400 degrees before doing anything else.
- Boil your pasta in water and salt for 6 mins then remove all the liquids.
- Now begin to stir fry your onions, in butter, until they are soft then add the flour and milk slowly.

- Stir the mix until it is all smooth then add: the mustard, salt, poultry seasoning, and pepper.
- Let the mix heat until it becomes thick. Then continue to stir as the mix cooks.
- Once everything is thick shut the heat and add in your pimento and 2/3 C. of cheese.
- Let the mix cook until the cheese is melted then add in your mushrooms.
- Get a casserole dish and layer your pasta in the bottom of it then place some turkey and cover everything with the cheese sauce.
- Continue laying in this manner until all the ingredients have been used up.
- Now top the layers with the rest of the cheese which should be about 1/3 of a C.
- Cook the contents in the oven for 30 mins.
- Enjoy.

Amount per serving (6 total)

Timing Information:

Preparation	25 m
Cooking	25 m
Total Time	50 m

Nutritional Information:

Calories	604 kcal
Fat	26.4 g
Carbohydrates	52.1g
Protein	38.9 g
Cholesterol	113 mg
Sodium	914 mg

* Percent Daily Values are based on a 2,000 calorie diet.

AUTHENTIC CALAMARI

Ingredients

- 12 calamari tubes, cleaned and dried
- 2 green onions, finely diced
- 6 cloves garlic, minced
- 1/2 lb diced cooked shrimp meat
- 1/2 lb cooked crabmeat, diced
- 1 tbsp lemon juice
- 3/4 C. butter
- 12 oz. cream cheese, cut into cubes
- 2 cloves garlic, minced
- 3 C. milk
- 10 oz. freshly grated Parmesan cheese
- 1 pinch ground black pepper
- 3/4 C. freshly grated Romano cheese
- 1 (8 oz.) package linguine pasta

Directions

- Set your oven to 350 degrees before doing anything else.
- Get a bowl, combine: lemon juice, onions, crabmeat, 6 pieces of garlic, and shrimp.

- Divide this mix amongst your tubes of squid then stake the tubes closed with a toothpick.
- Place everything into a casserole dish.
- Begin to heat and stir 2 cloves of garlic and cream cheese in butter until the cheese is melted.
- Slowly add in your milk and keep stirring until all the milk is hot and everything is smooth.
- Now add the pepper and parmesan.
- Top the contents of the casserole dish with this mix. Then add 2 tbsp of Romano over everything.
- Cook the mix in the oven until the cheese has melted and is browned.
- At the same time begin to boil your pasta in water and salt for 9 mins then remove the liquid.
- Serve the calamad over the pasta with a liber amount of sauce.
- Enjoy.

Amount per serving (6 total)

Timing Information:

Preparation	20 m
Cooking	20 m
Total Time	40 m

Nutritional Information:

Calories	1019 kcal
Fat	65.6 g
Carbohydrates	141.7g
Protein	65.6 g
Cholesterol	1479 mg
Sodium	11549 mg

* Percent Daily Values are based on a 2,000 calorie diet.

CLASSICAL FETTUCCINE

Ingredients

- 8 oz. dry fettuccine pasta
- 3 cloves garlic
- 1/2 sweet onion, cut into wedges
- 3 tbsps fresh oregano leaves
- 4 tbsps olive oil
- 4 medium tomatoes, diced
- 3 tbsps diced fresh basil
- salt and pepper to taste
- 1 C. spinach leaves
- 1 lb cooked shrimp - peeled and deveined
- 8 oz. fresh mozzarella cheese, diced

Directions

- Cook your pasta in water and salt for 9 mins then remove all the liquids.
- Pulse the following a few times with a food processor: oregano, onion, and garlic.
- Once the mix is minced begin to stir fry it in olive oil until everything is browned then add in: the pepper, tomatoes, salt, and basil.

- Let the mix cook for 7 mins.
- Now add in the spinach to the mix and let everything wilt then combine in the shrimp.
- Get everything hot then add in the pasta and the mozzarella and stir the mix.
- Enjoy.

Amount per serving (4 total)

Timing Information:

Preparation	15 m
Cooking	15 m
Total Time	30 m

Nutritional Information:

Calories	651 kcal
Fat	28.5 g
Carbohydrates	52.2g
Protein	43.8 g
Cholesterol	266 mg
Sodium	357 mg

* Percent Daily Values are based on a 2,000 calorie diet.

PINK AND GREEN ITALIAN PASTA

Ingredients

- 8 oz. dry fettuccine pasta
- 1/4 C. butter
- 1 C. milk
- 1 tbsp all-purpose flour
- 1 C. freshly grated Parmesan cheese
- 1/2 lb smoked salmon, diced
- 1 C. diced fresh spinach
- 2 tbsps capers
- 1/4 C. diced sun-dried tomatoes
- 1/2 C. diced fresh oregano

Directions

- Boil your pasta in water and salt for 9 mins then remove all the liquid.
- Begin to stir and heat your milk and butter in a large pot then once it is hot add in the flour and get everything thick.
- Slowly add in the parmesan and continue heating it until the cheese melts.

- Break the fish into the parmesan mix then add: the oregano, spinach, sun-dried tomatoes, and capers.
- Let the mix simmer for 5 mins while stirring.
- Lay your pasta on a serving plate then liberally top it with the buttery sauce.
- Enjoy.

Amount per serving (4 total)

Timing Information:

Preparation	15 m
Cooking	25 m
Total Time	40 m

Nutritional Information:

Calories	512 kcal
Fat	22.6 g
Carbohydrates	49.4g
Protein	28.9 g
Cholesterol	66 mg
Sodium	1065 mg

* Percent Daily Values are based on a 2,000 calorie diet.

Maggie's Easy Puttanesca (Southern Italian Style)

Ingredients

- 8 oz. pasta
- 1/2 C. olive oil
- 3 cloves garlic, minced
- 2 C. diced tomatoes, pushed through a sieve
- 4 anchovy filets, rinsed and diced
- 2 tbsps tomato paste
- 3 tbsps capers
- 20 Greek olives, pitted and coarsely diced
- 1/2 tsp crushed red pepper flakes

Directions

- Boil your pasta in water and salt for 9 mins then remove all the liquids.
- Now being to stir fry your garlic in oil until it is browned all over.
- Then add the tomatoes and cook the mix for 7 mins before adding in: the pepper flakes, anchovies, olives, tomato paste, and capers.

- Let the mix cook for 12 mins and stir everything at least 2 times.
- Now add in the pasta and stir everything to evenly coat the noodles.
- Enjoy.

Amount per serving (4 total)

Timing Information:

Preparation	25 m
Cooking	15 m
Total Time	40 m

Nutritional Information:

Calories	490 kcal
Fat	34 g
Carbohydrates	38.7g
Protein	9.3 g
Cholesterol	44 mg
Sodium	728 mg

* Percent Daily Values are based on a 2,000 calorie diet.

Classical Penne Pasta

Ingredients

- 1 (16 oz.) package penne pasta
- 2 tbsps olive oil
- 1/4 C. diced red onion
- 1 tbsp diced garlic
- 1/4 C. white wine
- 2 (14.5 oz.) cans diced tomatoes
- 1 lb shrimp, peeled and deveined
- 1 C. grated Parmesan cheese

Directions

- Boil your pasta in water and salt for 9 mins then remove the liquids.
- Now begin to stir fry your garlic and onions in oil until the onions are soft.
- Then add in the tomatoes and wine.
- Simmer the mix for 12 mins while stirring. Then add in the shrimp and cook everything for 6 mins.
- Now add the pasta and stir everything to evenly coat the noodles.
- Enjoy.

Amount per serving (8 total)

Timing Information:

Preparation	10 m
Cooking	25 m
Total Time	35 m

Nutritional Information:

Calories	385 kcal
Fat	8.5 g
Carbohydrates	48.5g
Protein	24.5 g
Cholesterol	95 mg
Sodium	399 mg

* Percent Daily Values are based on a 2,000 calorie diet.

Parmesan Orzo

Ingredients

- 1/2 C. butter, divided
- 8 pearl onions
- 1 C. uncooked orzo pasta
- 1/2 C. sliced fresh mushrooms
- 1 C. water
- 1/2 C. white wine
- garlic powder to taste
- salt and pepper to taste
- 1/2 C. grated Parmesan cheese
- 1/4 C. fresh parsley

Directions

- Stir fry your onions in half of the butter until it is browned then add in the rest of the butter, mushrooms, and the orzo.
- Continue frying everything for 7 mins.
- Now combine in the wine and the water and get everything boiling.

- Once the mix is boiling, set the heat to low, and cook everything for 9 mins after adding in the pepper, salt and garlic powder.
- Once the orzo is done top it with parsley and parmesan.
- Enjoy.

Amount per serving (6 total)

Timing Information:

Preparation	15 m
Cooking	25 m
Total Time	40 m

Nutritional Information:

Calories	327 kcal
Fat	18.6 g
Carbohydrates	28.1g
Protein	8.6 g
Cholesterol	48 mg
Sodium	306 mg

* Percent Daily Values are based on a 2,000 calorie diet.

PASTA RUSTIC

Ingredients

- 1 lb farfalle (bow tie) pasta
- 1/3 C. olive oil
- 1 clove garlic, chopped
- 1/4 C. butter
- 2 small zucchini, quartered and sliced
- 1 onion, chopped
- 1 tomato, chopped
- 1 (8 oz) package mushrooms, sliced
- 1 tbsp dried oregano
- 1 tbsp paprika
- salt and pepper to taste

Directions

- Boil your pasta for 10 mins in water and salt. Remove excess liquid and set aside.
- Fry your salt, pepper, garlic, paprika, zucchini, oregano, mushrooms, onion, and tomato, for 17 mins in olive oil.
- Mix the veggies and pasta.
- Enjoy.

Servings: 4 servings

Timing Information:

Preparation	Cooking	Total Time
10 mins	25 mins	35 mins

Nutritional Information:

Calories	717 kcal
Carbohydrates	92.8 g
Cholesterol	31 mg
Fat	32.9 g
Fiber	7.5 g
Protein	18.1 g
Sodium	491 mg

* Percent Daily Values are based on a 2,000 calorie diet.

Simple Pesto

Ingredients

- 1/4 C. almonds
- 3 cloves garlic
- 1 1/2 C. fresh basil leaves
- 1/2 C. olive oil
- 1 pinch ground nutmeg
- salt and pepper to taste

Directions

- Set your oven to 450 degrees F before doing anything else.
- Arrange the almonds onto a cookie sheet and bake for about 10 minutes or till toasted slightly.
- In a food processor, add the toasted almonds and the remaining ingredients till a rough paste forms.

Amount per serving (6 total)

Timing Information:

Preparation	2 m
Cooking	10 m
Total Time	12 m

Nutritional Information:

Calories	199 kcal
Fat	21.1 g
Carbohydrates	2g
Protein	1.7 g
Cholesterol	0 mg
Sodium	389 mg

* Percent Daily Values are based on a 2,000 calorie diet.

CHEESY ARTICHOKE PESTO

Ingredients

- 2 C. fresh basil leaves
- 2 tbsps crumbled feta cheese
- 1/4 C. freshly grated Parmesan cheese
- 1/4 C. pine nuts, toasted
- 1 artichoke heart, roughly chopped
- 2 tbsps chopped oil-packed sun-dried tomatoes
- 1/2 C. extra-virgin olive oil
- 1 pinch salt and black pepper to taste

Directions

- In a large food processor, add all the ingredients except the oil and seasoning and pulse till combined.
- While the motor is running slowly, add the oil and pulse till smooth.
- Season with salt and black pepper and serve.

Amount per serving (12 total)

Timing Information:

Preparation	
Cooking	5 m
Total Time	5 m

Nutritional Information:

Calories	118 kcal
Fat	11.9 g
Carbohydrates	1.1g
Protein	2 g
Cholesterol	3 mg
Sodium	92 mg

* Percent Daily Values are based on a 2,000 calorie diet.

AMERICAN PESTO

Ingredients

- 4 C. packed fresh basil leaves
- 1/4 C. Italian parsley
- 2 cloves garlic, peeled and lightly crushed
- 1 C. pine nuts
- 1 1/2 C. shredded Parmigiano-Reggiano cheese
- 1 tbsp fresh lemon juice
- 1/2 C. extra-virgin olive oil, or more as needed
- salt and ground black pepper to taste

Directions

- In a food processor, add the parsley, basil, and garlic and pulse till chopped finely.
- Add the pine nuts and pulse till copped very finely as well.
- Add the cheese and pulse till combined.
- While the motor is running, slowly mix in the lemon juice.
- Then add the oil and pulse till well combined and smooth.
- Season with salt and black pepper and serve.

Amount per serving (6 total)

Timing Information:

Preparation	
Cooking	15 m
Total Time	15 m

Nutritional Information:

Calories	389 kcal
Fat	35.8 g
Carbohydrates	5.4g
Protein	14.1 g
Cholesterol	14 mg
Sodium	343 mg

* Percent Daily Values are based on a 2,000 calorie diet.

Pasta Pesto

Ingredients

- 4 C. fresh baby spinach
- 1/2 C. pecans
- 2 cloves garlic
- 1 C. Parmesan cheese
- 1 tbsp lemon juice
- 1/2 C. extra virgin olive oil
- 1 pinch salt and freshly ground black pepper to taste

Directions

- In a large food processor, add all the ingredients except the oil and pulse till combined.
- While the motor is running slowly, add the oil and pulse till well combined and smooth.

Amount per serving (16 total)

Timing Information:

Preparation	
Cooking	10 m
Total Time	10 m

Nutritional Information:

Calories	113 kcal
Fat	11.1 g
Carbohydrates	1.2g
Protein	2.5 g
Cholesterol	4 mg
Sodium	82 mg

* Percent Daily Values are based on a 2,000 calorie diet.

ASIAN PEANUT PESTO

Ingredients

- 1 bunch cilantro
- 1/4 C. peanut butter
- 3 cloves garlic, diced
- 3 tbsps extra-virgin olive oil
- 2 tbsps diced fresh ginger
- 1 1/2 tbsps fish sauce
- 1 tbsp brown sugar
- 1/2 tsp cayenne pepper

Directions

- In a blender or food processor, add all the ingredients and pulse till smooth.

Amount per serving (10 total)

Timing Information:

Preparation	
Cooking	10 m
Total Time	10 m

Nutritional Information:

Calories	84 kcal
Fat	7.4 g
Carbohydrates	3.4g
Protein	1.9 g
Cholesterol	0 mg
Sodium	197 mg

* Percent Daily Values are based on a 2,000 calorie diet.

PESTO SPIRALS

Ingredients

- 1 tbsp olive oil
- 4 small zucchini, cut into noodle-shape strands
- 1/2 C. drained and rinsed canned garbanzo beans (chickpeas)
- 3 tbsps pesto, or to taste
- salt and ground black pepper to taste
- 2 tbsps shredded white Cheddar cheese, or to taste

Directions

- In a skillet, heat oil on medium heat.
- Stir in the zucchini and cook for about 5-10 minutes or till all the liquid is absorbed.
- Stir in the pesto and chickpeas and immediately reduce the heat to medium-low and cook for about 5 minutes or till the chickpeas and zucchini noodles are coated completely.
- Stir in the salt and black pepper and immediately place the zucchini mixture onto serving plates.
- Garnish the dish with the cheese and serve immediately.

Amount per serving (2 total)

Timing Information:

Preparation	10 m
Cooking	10 m
Total Time	20 m

Nutritional Information:

Calories	319 kcal
Fat	21.3 g
Carbohydrates	23.1g
Protein	12.1 g
Cholesterol	16 mg
Sodium	511 mg

* Percent Daily Values are based on a 2,000 calorie diet.

SPICY PESTO

Ingredients

- 1/4 C. walnuts
- 2 cloves garlic
- 2 C. packed fresh basil leaves
- 3/4 C. shredded Parmagiano-Reggiano cheese
- 1 jalapeno pepper, stem removed
- 2/3 C. olive oil
- salt and ground black pepper to taste

Directions

- In a food processor, add the garlic and walnuts and pulse till chopped finely.
- Add the jalapeno, basil and cheese and pulse till well combined.
- While the motor is running slowly, add the oil and pulse till well combined and smooth.
- Season with salt and black pepper and serve.

Amount per serving (14 total)

Timing Information:

Preparation	
Cooking	10 m
Total Time	10 m

Nutritional Information:

Calories	126 kcal
Fat	13 g
Carbohydrates	0.8g
Protein	2.2 g
Cholesterol	4 mg
Sodium	66 mg

* Percent Daily Values are based on a 2,000 calorie diet.

MUSHROOM PESTO

Ingredients

- 2 tbsps butter
- 1 lb mixed fresh mushrooms (such as cremini, button, oyster, and portobello), quartered
- 1 shallot, chopped
- 1 C. toasted pine nuts
- 1/4 C. extra-virgin olive oil
- 1/4 C. vegetable broth
- 3 cloves garlic, chopped
- 1 tbsp freshly squeezed lemon juice
- 1 tsp kosher salt
- 1/2 tsp freshly ground black pepper
- 1/2 C. Parmesan cheese, grated

Directions

- In a pan, melt the butter on medium heat.
- Stir in the shallots and mushrooms and cook for about 5-7 minutes or till the mushrooms become golden brown.
- Remove from heat and keep aside to cool for about 10 minutes.

- In a blender, add the cooked mushroom mixture and remaining ingredients except cheese and pulse till grounded finely.
- Transfer the mixture into a bowl and stir in the cheese before serving.

Amount per serving (6 total)

Timing Information:

Preparation	15 m
Cooking	15 m
Total Time	30 m

Nutritional Information:

Calories	302 kcal
Fat	26.9 g
Carbohydrates	8.4g
Protein	10.8 g
Cholesterol	16 mg
Sodium	474 mg

* Percent Daily Values are based on a 2,000 calorie diet.

CREAMY LETTUCE PESTO

Ingredients

- 1/2 clove garlic
- 1/3 C. walnuts
- 3 oz. watercress, rinsed and dried
- 1 C. freshly grated Parmesan cheese
- 2 tbsps mayonnaise

Directions

- In a food processor, add all the ingredients and pulse till a smooth paste forms.

Amount per serving (8 total)

Timing Information:

Preparation	
Cooking	10 m
Total Time	10 m

Nutritional Information:

Calories	113 kcal
Fat	9.6 g
Carbohydrates	1.5g
Protein	5.9 g
Cholesterol	12 mg
Sodium	215 mg

* Percent Daily Values are based on a 2,000 calorie diet.

NUTTY PESTO

Ingredients

- 2 C. basil leaves
- 1/2 C. walnuts
- 1/4 C. olive oil
- 2 cloves garlic
- 1 tbsp lemon juice

Directions

- In a food processor, add all the ingredients and pulse till a smooth paste forms.

Amount per serving (2 total)

Timing Information:

Preparation	
Cooking	10 m
Total Time	10 m

Nutritional Information:

Calories	455 kcal
Fat	47.3 g
Carbohydrates	6.9g
Protein	6.1 g
Cholesterol	0 mg
Sodium	3 mg

* Percent Daily Values are based on a 2,000 calorie diet.

CREAMY & CHEESY PESTO SHRIMP WITH PASTA

Ingredients

- 1 lb linguine pasta
- 1/2 C. butter
- 2 C. heavy cream
- 1/2 tsp ground black pepper
- 1 C. grated Parmesan cheese
- 1/3 C. pesto
- 1 lb large shrimp, peeled and deveined

Directions

- In a large pan of lightly salted boiling water, add the pasta and cook for about 8-10 minutes or till desired doneness and drain well and keep aside.
- Meanwhile, melt the butter in a large skillet on medium heat.
- Add the cream and black pepper and cook, stirring continuously for about 6-8 minutes.
- Add the cheese and stir till well combined.
- Stir in the pesto and cook, stirring continuously for about 3-5 minutes.

- Add the shrimp and cook for about 3-5 minutes.
- Serve hot with pasta.

Amount per serving (8 total)

Timing Information:

Preparation	15 m
Cooking	15 m
Total Time	30 m

Nutritional Information:

Calories	646 kcal
Fat	42.5 g
Carbohydrates	43g
Protein	23.1 g
Cholesterol	210 mg
Sodium	437 mg

* Percent Daily Values are based on a 2,000 calorie diet.

Cheesy Pesto Chicken & Pasta Bake

Ingredients

- 1/2 C. seasoned bread crumbs
- 1/2 C. grated Parmesan cheese
- 1 tbsp olive oil
- 1 (16 oz.) box penne pasta
- 6 C. cubed cooked chicken
- 4 C. shredded Italian cheese blend
- 3 C. fresh baby spinach
- 1 (15 oz.) can crushed tomatoes
- 1 (15 oz.) jar Alfredo sauce
- 1 (15 oz.) jar pesto sauce
- 1 1/2 C. milk

Directions

- Set your oven to 350 degrees F before doing anything else and coat a 13x9-inch baking dish with cooking spray.
- In a small bowl, add the Parmesan cheese, breadcrumbs and oil and mix till well combined and keep aside.
- In a large pan of lightly salted boiling water, add the pasta and cook for about 10-11 minutes or till desired doneness and drain well and keep aside.

- In the same time in a large bowl, add the remaining ingredients and mix then stir in the pasta.
- Lay the chicken mixture onto the prepared baking dish evenly and spread the Parmesan mixture on top evenly.
- Cook the dish in the oven for 40-45 minutes or till the top becomes golden brown and bubbly.

Amount per serving (12 total)

Timing Information:

Preparation	15 m
Cooking	1 h
Total Time	1 h 15 m

Nutritional Information:

Calories	760 kcal
Fat	47.2 g
Carbohydrates	40.7g
Protein	45.4 g
Cholesterol	114 mg
Sodium	1210 mg

* Percent Daily Values are based on a 2,000 calorie diet.

PASTA WITH PESTO CHICKEN & SPINACH

Ingredients

- 2 tbsps olive oil
- 2 cloves garlic, finely chopped
- 4 skinless, boneless chicken breast halves - cut into strips
- 2 C. fresh spinach leaves
- 1 (4.5 oz.) package dry Alfredo sauce mix
- 2 tbsps pesto
- 1 (8 oz.) package dry penne pasta
- 1 tbsp grated Romano cheese

Directions

- In a large skillet, heat oil on medium-high heat and sauté garlic for about 1 minute.
- Add the chicken and cook for about 7-8 minutes from both sides and stir in the spinach and cook for about 3-4 minutes.
- At the same time, prepare the Alfredo sauce according to the package's directions and add the pesto and stir to combine and keep aside.

- In a large pan of lightly salted boiling water, add the pasta and cook for about 8-10 minutes or till desired doneness and drain well.
- In a large bowl, add the cooked pasta, chicken mixture and pesto mixture and toss to coat well.
- Serve immediately with a garnishing of cheese.

Amount per serving (4 total)

Timing Information:

Preparation	20 m
Cooking	35 m
Total Time	55 m

Nutritional Information:

Calories	572 kcal
Fat	19.3 g
Carbohydrates	57.3g
Protein	41.9 g
Cholesterol	84 mg
Sodium	1707 mg

* Percent Daily Values are based on a 2,000 calorie diet.

PASTA WITH CHEESY PESTO SHRIMP & MUSHROOMS

Ingredients

- 1 (16 oz.) package linguine pasta
- 2 tbsps olive oil
- 1 small onion, chopped
- 8 cloves garlic, sliced
- 1/2 C. butter
- 2 tbsps all-purpose flour
- 2 C. milk
- 1 pinch salt
- 1 pinch pepper
- 1 1/2 C. grated Romano cheese
- 1 C. prepared basil pesto
- 1 lb cooked shrimp, peeled and deveined
- 20 mushrooms, chopped
- 3 roma (plum) tomato, diced

Directions

- In a large pan of lightly salted boiling water, add the pasta and cook for about 8-10 minutes or till desired doneness and drain well and keep aside.
- In a large skillet, heat oil on medium heat and sauté the onion for about 4-5 minutes.
- Add the butter and garlic and sauté for about 1 minute.
- Meanwhile in a bowl, mix together milk and flour and pour into a skillet, stirring continuously.
- Stir in the salt and black pepper and cook, stirring for about 4 minutes.
- Add the cheese, stirring continuously till melted completely.
- Stir in the pesto and shrimp, tomatoes and mushrooms and cook for about 4 minutes or till heated completely.
- Add the pasta and toss to coat and serve immediately.

Amount per serving (8 total)

Timing Information:

Preparation	30 m
Cooking	20 m
Total Time	50 m

Nutritional Information:

Calories	677 kcal
Fat	38.3 g
Carbohydrates	52.2g
Protein	33.6 g
Cholesterol	155 mg
Sodium	719 mg

* Percent Daily Values are based on a 2,000 calorie diet.

Parmesan Pesto

Ingredients

- 1 (16 oz.) package penne pasta
- 2 tbsps butter
- 2 tbsps olive oil
- 4 skinless, boneless chicken breast halves - cut into thin strips
- 2 cloves garlic, diced
- salt and pepper to taste
- 1 1/4 C. heavy cream
- 1/4 C. pesto
- 3 tbsps grated Parmesan cheese

Directions

- In a large pan of lightly salted boiling water, add the pasta and cook for about 8-10 minutes or till desired doneness and drain well and keep aside.
- In a large skillet, heat oil and butter on medium heat and cook the chicken for about 5-6 minutes or till almost done.
- Reduce the heat to medium-low and stir in the remaining ingredients and cook till the chicken is done completely.

- Add the pasta and toss to coat well and serve immediately.

Amount per serving (8 total)

Timing Information:

Preparation	20 m
Cooking	10 m
Total Time	30 m

Nutritional Information:

Calories	497 kcal
Fat	26.1 g
Carbohydrates	42.6g
Protein	24 g
Cholesterol	97 mg
Sodium	164 mg

* Percent Daily Values are based on a 2,000 calorie diet.

Brazilian Pesto

Ingredients

- 3 C. chopped fresh basil
- 1 C. extra virgin olive oil
- 1/2 C. pine nuts
- 1/8 C. Brazil nuts
- 2/3 C. grated Parmesan cheese
- 2 tbsps diced garlic
- 1/2 tsp chili powder

Directions

- In a food processor, add all the ingredients except oil and pulse till a thick paste forms.
- While the motor is running slowly, add the oil and pulse till smooth.

Amount per serving (12 total)

Timing Information:

Preparation	
Cooking	15 m
Total Time	15 m

Nutritional Information:

Calories	234 kcal
Fat	23.9 g
Carbohydrates	1.9g
Protein	3.7 g
Cholesterol	4 mg
Sodium	70 mg

* Percent Daily Values are based on a 2,000 calorie diet.

Mozzarella Pesto Salad

Ingredients

- 1 1/2 C. rotini pasta
- 3 tbsps pesto, or to taste
- 1 tbsp extra-virgin olive oil
- 1/4 tsp salt, or to taste
- 1/4 tsp granulated garlic
- 1/8 tsp ground black pepper
- 1/2 C. halved grape tomatoes
- 1/2 C. small (pearlini) fresh mozzarella balls
- 2 leaves fresh basil leaves, finely shredded

Directions

- In a large pan of lightly salted boiling water, add the pasta and cook for about 8 minutes or till desired doneness and drain well and keep aside.
- In a large bowl, mix together pesto, granulated garlic, oil, salt and black pepper and add the pasta and toss to coat.
- Gently, fold in the mozzarella, tomatoes and basil and serve immediately.

Amount per serving (6 total)

Timing Information:

Preparation	10 m
Cooking	10 m
Total Time	20 m

Nutritional Information:

Calories	169 kcal
Fat	8.3 g
Carbohydrates	17.1g
Protein	6.1 g
Cholesterol	10 mg
Sodium	173 mg

* Percent Daily Values are based on a 2,000 calorie diet.

PESTO WALNUT PASTA

Ingredients

- olive oil
- 2 lbs fresh spinach, cleaned
- 2 lbs nonfat ricotta cheese
- 4 large cloves garlic, diced
- 1/2 tsp salt
- Freshly ground black pepper to taste
- 1/2 C. grated Parmesan cheese
- 1/3 C. diced walnuts, lightly toasted
- 1 (24 oz.) jar tomato sauce
- 16 fresh, uncooked lasagna noodles
- 1/2 lb mozzarella, grated

Walnut Pesto:
- 3 C. packed fresh basil leaves
- 3 large cloves garlic
- 1/3 C. lightly toasted walnuts
- 1/3 C. extra virgin olive oil
- 1/3 C. grated Parmesan cheese
- Salt and pepper to taste
- Additional extra-virgin olive oil (for storage)

Directions

- Set your oven to 350 degrees F before doing anything else and coat a 13x9-inch casserole dish with some cooking spray.
- For the pesto, in a food processor, add basil, garlic and walnuts and pulse till chopped finely.
- While the motor is running slowly, add the oil and pulse till smooth and transfer into a bowl and mix in the parmesan, salt and black pepper.
- In a large bowl, mix together the cottage or ricotta cheese, half of the parmesan, pesto, spinach, garlic, walnuts, salt and black pepper.
- Place half of the tomato sauce in the bottom of the prepared baking dish and place 1 layer of uncooked lasagna noodles over the tomato sauce.
- Place one-third of the spinach mixture over the noodles, followed by 1/3 of the mozzarella.
- Repeat the layers once, and finish up with the last layer of noodles.
- Cover and cook in the oven for about 35 minutes.
- Uncover the casserole dish and sprinkle the top of the lasagna with the reserved Parmesan cheese and cook for 15 minutes more.

Amount per serving (8 total)

Timing Information:

Preparation	30 m
Cooking	1 h
Total Time	1 h 30 m

Nutritional Information:

Calories	638 kcal
Fat	27.2 g
Carbohydrates	64.3g
Protein	32.6 g
Cholesterol	45 mg
Sodium	1025 mg

* Percent Daily Values are based on a 2,000 calorie diet.

PASTA WITH PESTO VEGGIES

Ingredients

- 1 C. fresh basil leaves
- 2 cloves garlic, diced
- 1/4 C. pine nuts
- 1/2 C. Parmesan cheese
- 1/4 C. olive oil
- 2 tbsps lemon juice
- 4 C. mini penne pasta
- 1 tbsp olive oil
- 1 tbsp olive oil
- 1/4 C. pine nuts
- 1 C. chopped asparagus
- 1/2 C. sliced zucchini
- 1/2 C. sliced Kalamata olives
- 1/2 C. diced roasted red pepper
- 1/2 C. chopped sun-dried tomatoes
- 1/2 C. grated Parmesan cheese

Directions

- In a large pan of lightly salted boiling water, add the pasta and cook for about 11 minutes or till desired doneness and drain well and transfer into a bowl with 1 tbsp of oil and keep aside.

- Meanwhile in a food processor, add basil, garlic, 1/2 C. of cheese, 1/4 C. of oil, 1/4 C. of pine nuts and lemon juice and pulse till smooth and keep aside.
- In a large skillet, heat the remaining oil on medium heat and cook the remaining 1/4 C. of pine nuts.
- Cook till golden brown and transfer onto a plate and keep aside.
- In the same skillet, add the remaining ingredients except the cheese and cook for about 5-7 minutes and stir in the pine nuts.
- Add the desired amount of pesto and pasta and toss to combine.
- Serve immediately with a garnishing of cheese.

Amount per serving (8 total)

Timing Information:

Preparation	20 m
Cooking	20 m
Total Time	40 m

Nutritional Information:

Calories	367 kcal
Fat	20.6 g
Carbohydrates	34.4g
Protein	12.6 g
Cholesterol	9 mg
Sodium	413 mg

* Percent Daily Values are based on a 2,000 calorie diet.

No-Noodle Lasagna

Ingredients

- 1 lb ground beef
- 1 (26 oz) jar spaghetti sauce
- 1/2 tsp garlic powder
- 3 C. cooked rice, cooled
- 2 eggs, lightly beaten
- 3/4 C. shredded Parmesan cheese, divided
- 2 1/4 C. shredded mozzarella cheese
- 2 C. cottage cheese

Directions

- Set your oven to 375 degrees before doing anything else.
- Fry your beef until browned for 8 mins, and remove excess grease. Combine in your tomato sauce and also garlic powder.
- Get a bowl, mix: 1/4 C. parmesan, whisked eggs, and rice.
- Get a 2nd bowl, mix: 1/4 C. parmesan, cottage cheese, and 2 C. mozzarella
- Layer the following in a dish: 1/2 rice, 1/2 cheese mix, 1/2 meat. Continue until dish is full. Then top with more mozzarella.
- Cook for 25 mins, until sauce is simmering, and cheese melted.

Servings: 8 servings

Timing Information:

Preparation	Cooking	Total Time
20 mins	25 mins	45 mins

Nutritional Information:

Calories	461 kcal
Carbohydrates	35.3 g
Cholesterol	118 mg
Fat	20.3 g
Fiber	2.6 g
Protein	32 g
Sodium	975 mg

* Percent Daily Values are based on a 2,000 calorie diet.

No-Bake 3 Cheese Lasagna

Ingredients

- 1 (16 oz) package lasagna noodles
- 1 lb lean ground beef
- 1 1/2 (26 oz) jars spaghetti sauce
- 2 C. shredded mozzarella cheese
- 1/2 C. grated Parmesan cheese
- 1 (8 oz) container ricotta cheese
- 2 eggs
- 2 C. shredded mozzarella cheese

Directions

- Boil lasagna in salted water for 7 min until al dente. Remove all water.
- Fry your beef until brown, remove oil excess, mix in tomato sauce, simmer for 5 mins. Turn off heat.
- Get a bowl, mix: beaten eggs, 2 C. mozzarella, ricotta, and parmesan.
- Place half of your beef into the slow cooker first, then some lasagna noodles. Then 1/4 of the cheese mix, then 1/4 more sauce. Continue adding layers until nothing is lest. Topmost layer should be 2 C. of mozzarella.
- Set slow cooker to high for 3 hours. Then set heat to low for 8 hours.
- Enjoy.

Servings: 10 servings

Timing Information:

Preparation	Cooking	Total Time
30 mins	2 hrs	2 hrs 30 mins

Nutritional Information:

Calories	521 kcal
Carbohydrates	50.3 g
Cholesterol	110 mg
Fat	20.6 g
Fiber	4.4 g
Protein	33.1 g
Sodium	861 mg

* Percent Daily Values are based on a 2,000 calorie diet.

Garden Lasagna III
(Broccoli, Carrots, & Corn)

Ingredients

- 1 box lasagna noodles
- 2 eggs, beaten
- 1 box part-skim ricotta cheese
- 2 cans condensed cream of mushroom soup
- 2 C. shredded Cheddar cheese
- 1 C. grated Parmesan cheese
- 1 C. sour cream
- 1 package herb and garlic soup mix
- 1 bag chopped frozen broccoli, thawed
- 1 bag frozen sliced carrots
- 1 bag frozen corn kernels

Directions

- Set your oven to 375 degrees before anything else.
- Boil noodles in water with salt for 10 mins. Remove all water, set aside.
- Get a bowl, mix: soup mix, beaten eggs, sour cream, ricotta, parmesan, cheddar, and mushroom soup.
- In your baking layer everything in the following manner: lasagna, cheese mix, carrots, corn, broccoli. Continue until all ingredients used. Cheese should be upmost layer.

- Cook for 30, with a cover of foil. 10 mins without.
- Enjoy.

Servings: 8 to 10 servings

Timing Information:

Preparation	Cooking	Total Time
30 mins	40 mins	1 hr 10 mins

Nutritional Information:

Calories	534 kcal
Carbohydrates	48.8 g
Cholesterol	103 mg
Fat	27 g
Fiber	4.3 g
Protein	26.6 g
Sodium	1091 mg

* Percent Daily Values are based on a 2,000 calorie diet.

Pretty Easy Lasagna

Ingredients

- 2 C. uncooked penne pasta
- 1 lb ground Italian sausage
- 1 (26 oz) jar spaghetti sauce
- 1 C. cottage cheese
- 2 C. shredded mozzarella cheese, divided

Directions

- Set your oven to 350 degrees before doing anything else.
- Boil your pasta for 8 mins in water and salt. While stir frying your Italian sausage for 10 mins. Then remove oil excesses. Combine pasta, and tomato sauce, with your sausage. And simmer the mix for 3 mins.
- Now coat a baking dish with nonstick spray. And layer 1/2 of the sauce and pasta at the bottom. Add a layer of cottage cheese, 1/2 mozzarella, add the rest of the pasta. Finally add the rest of the mozzarella.
- Bake for 30 mins covered with foil. 5 mins without a covering.
- Enjoy.

Servings: 8 servings

Timing Information:

Preparation	Cooking	Total Time
15 mins	25 mins	40 mins

Nutritional Information:

Calories	386 kcal
Carbohydrates	29.6 g
Cholesterol	46 mg
Fat	19.3 g
Fiber	3.2 g
Protein	22.1 g
Sodium	1135 mg

* Percent Daily Values are based on a 2,000 calorie diet.

Microwave Mexican Lasagna

Ingredients

- 11 oz lasagna noodles
- 1 lb lean ground beef
- 24 oz tomato sauce
- 1/2 C. water
- 1 (1 oz) package taco seasoning mix
- 8 C. shredded Cheddar cheese
- 1/2 C. minced tortilla chips

Directions

- Boil your pasta for 10 mins in water and salt. Remove all water. Set aside.
- Fry your beef until browned, and remove excess oils. Combine in some taco seasoning, then tomato and finally water. Lightly simmer for 6 mins.
- Get your dish (must be able to fit in microwave), and layer in the following manner: lasagna noodles, beef mix, cheese. Continue until dish is full.
- Microwave for 10 mins on the highest power setting covered with plastic wrap.
- Garnish with tortilla chips.
- Enjoy.

Servings: 8 to 10 servings

Timing Information:

Preparation	Cooking	Total Time
10 mins	10 mins	25 mins

Nutritional Information:

Calories	709 kcal
Carbohydrates	35.8 g
Cholesterol	143 mg
Fat	45.4 g
Fiber	2.3 g
Protein	39.3 g
Sodium	1304 mg

* Percent Daily Values are based on a 2,000 calorie diet.

EASY CHEDDAR LASAGNA

Ingredients

- 1 (16 oz) package lasagna noodles
- 1 lb lean ground beef
- salt and pepper to taste
- 1 (16 oz) jar spaghetti sauce
- 1 clove garlic, minced
- 1/2 lb shredded mozzarella cheese
- 1/2 lb shredded Cheddar cheese
- 1 pint ricotta cheese

Directions

- Set your oven to 350 degrees before doing anything else.
- Get a bowl mix: ricotta, mozzarella, and cheddar.
- Boil your noodles in water and salt for 9 mins. Remove water. Set aside
- Fry your beef seasoned with pepper and salt, until cooked. Remove oil excess. Combine in garlic and tomato sauce. Simmer for 6 mins.
- In your baking dish layer: noodles, meat, and then cheese. Continue until dish is full.
- Cook for 30 mins.
- Enjoy.

Servings: 1 pan

Timing Information:

Preparation	Cooking	Total Time
30 mins	30 mins	1 hr

Nutritional Information:

Calories	643 kcal
Carbohydrates	53.4 g
Cholesterol	108 mg
Fat	29.3 g
Fiber	3.4 g
Protein	41.3 g
Sodium	707 mg

* Percent Daily Values are based on a 2,000 calorie diet.

Cupcake Lasagnas

Ingredients

- nonstick spray
- 1 C. shredded mozzarella cheese
- 1 C. grated Asiago cheese
- 2 C. prepared pasta sauce
- 1/2 (16 oz) package wonton wrappers

Directions

- Set your oven to 375 degrees before doing anything else.
- Coat muffin tins with some nonstick spray.
- Get a bowl, mix: Asiago and mozzarella.
- Take your muffin tin and in each section put a wonton wrap.
- Fill each section halfway with sauce, then 2 and half tbsps of cheese, then add a new wonton wrap to each. Add sauce, and more cheese.
- Cook for 25 mins.
- Enjoy.

Servings: 12

Timing Information:

Preparation	Cooking	Total Time
15 mins	20 mins	35 mins

Nutritional Information:

Calories	147 kcal
Carbohydrates	16.8 g
Cholesterol	17 mg
Fat	5.5 g
Fiber	1.4 g
Protein	7.1 g
Sodium	445 mg

* Percent Daily Values are based on a 2,000 calorie diet.

Stovetop Lasagna

Ingredients

- 1 lb ground beef
- 4 C. water
- 3 beef bouillon cubes
- 7 dry lasagna noodles, split in half
- 1 (10.75 oz) can condensed tomato soup
- 1 onion, chopped
- 2 cloves garlic, minced
- 1 1/2 tbsps Italian seasoning
- 1/2 tsp ground black pepper
- 1 tsp cornstarch
- salt to taste

Directions

- Fry your beef for 10 mins and remove oils. Combine in some bouillon cubes, and water. Stir until cubes dissolve. Then bring everything to a boiling state. Put in noodles and the following: pepper, tomato soup, Italian seasoning, garlic, and onions. Lower the heat and simmer for 12 mins.
- Get a bowl and mix some cornstarch with one C. of sauce, then combine it back with the noodles. Simmer for another 3 to 5 mins.
- Enjoy after everything cools.

Servings: 4 servings

Timing Information:

Preparation	Cooking	Total Time
10 mins	35 mins	45 mins

Nutritional Information:

Calories	441 kcal
Carbohydrates	48.8 g
Cholesterol	69 mg
Fat	15.8 g
Fiber	3.5 g
Protein	27.2 g
Sodium	1148 mg

* Percent Daily Values are based on a 2,000 calorie diet.

Lasagna Alfredo

Ingredients

- 1 (16 oz) package lasagna noodles
- 2 tbsps olive oil
- 1 small onion, chopped
- 1 (16 oz) package frozen chopped spinach, thawed
- 7 oz basil pesto
- 30 oz ricotta cheese
- 1 egg
- 1/2 tsp salt
- 1/4 tsp ground black pepper
- 1/4 tsp ground nutmeg
- 2 C. mozzarella cheese, shredded
- 9 oz Alfredo-style pasta sauce
- 1/4 C. grated Parmesan cheese

Directions

- Set your oven to 350 degrees before doing anything else.
- Coat your baking dish with nonstick spray, or oil.
- Get a bowl, mix: whisked eggs, nutmeg, pepper, ricotta, and salt.
- Boil your pasta for 9 mins in salty water. Remove all liquid.
- Stir fry spinach and onions with olive oil. Until onions are soft. Turn off the heat then add in pesto.

- Add everything to a dish in the following manner: noodles, spinach, ricotta, mozzarella. Continue until everything is used. Garnish with some parmesan.
- Cook for 50 mins. While covered. Let everything sit for 10 mins.
- Enjoy.

Servings: 8 servings

Timing Information:

Preparation	Cooking	Total Time
35 mins	45 mins	1 hr 30 mins

Nutritional Information:

Calories	712 kcal
Carbohydrates	53.7 g
Cholesterol	98 mg
Fat	40.4 g
Fiber	4.4 g
Protein	36.6 g
Sodium	1071 mg

* Percent Daily Values are based on a 2,000 calorie diet.

Garden Lasagna III
(Asparagus)

Ingredients

- 5 lasagna noodles, halved
- 2 tbsps margarine
- 2 cloves garlic, chopped
- 2 tbsps all-purpose flour
- 1 1/2 C. milk
- 1/2 tsp dried thyme
- 1 (15 oz) can asparagus, drained
- 1 C. julienned fully cooked ham
- 1 C. shredded mozzarella cheese

Directions

- Boil your noodles for 9 mins in water and salt. Remove all water. Set aside.
- Stir fry your onions in melted butter, then add some flour and thyme. Continue stirring until everything is even and smooth. Add milk, and continue stirring. Lower heat and simmer for 10 mins until everything becomes sauce like. Set aside.
- Coat a baking dish (which can fit in the microwave) with nonstick spray or oil. Enter in your noodles, then some

sauce, ham, asparagus, and mozzarella. Continue layering in this process until dish is full or all ingredients used.

- For 10 mins microwave the lasagna covered with plastic. Increase the time if the cheese is not melted after 10 mins.
- Enjoy.

Servings: 4 servings

Timing Information:

Preparation	Cooking	Total Time
20 mins	10 mins	30 mins

Nutritional Information:

Calories	388 kcal
Carbohydrates	33.2 g
Cholesterol	44 mg
Fat	18.8 g
Fiber	2.3 g
Protein	22.6 g
Sodium	1008 mg

* Percent Daily Values are based on a 2,000 calorie diet.

Maggie's Favorite Lasagna

Ingredients

- 2 C. ricotta cheese
- 1 (10 oz) package frozen chopped spinach - thawed, drained and squeezed dry
- 1 1/2 C. grated Romano cheese
- 2 eggs
- salt and pepper to taste
- 1/4 C. spaghetti sauce
- 1 (25 oz) package frozen cheese ravioli
- 1/2 C. spaghetti sauce
- 1/2 C. grated Romano cheese

Directions

- Set your oven to 375 degrees before doing anything else.
- Get a bowl, mix: pepper, ricotta, salt, spinach, 1.5 C. Romano, and whisked eggs.
- Coat a dish with nonstick spray.
- Layer the following in your dish: 1/4 C. sauce, raviolis, 1 C. ricotta. Continue until dish is full. Add a topping of Romano.
- Cook for 40 mins covered with foil in the oven. Finally remove the foil and continue baking for 10 more mins.
- Enjoy.

Servings: 6 servings

Timing Information:

Preparation	Cooking	Total Time
10 mins	50 mins	1 hr 10 mins

Nutritional Information:

Calories	609 kcal
Carbohydrates	49.4 g
Cholesterol	175 mg
Fat	28.5 g
Fiber	5.5 g
Protein	39.6 g
Sodium	1025 mg

* Percent Daily Values are based on a 2,000 calorie diet.

THANKS FOR READING! JOIN THE CLUB AND KEEP ON COOKING WITH 6 MORE COOKBOOKS....

http://bit.ly/1TdrStv

 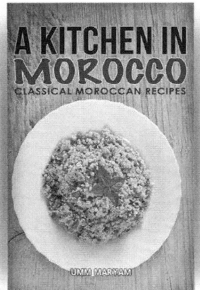 

To grab the box sets simply follow the link mentioned above, or tap one of book covers.

This will take you to a page where you can simply enter your email address and a PDF version of the box sets will be emailed to you.

Hope you are ready for some serious cooking!

http://bit.ly/1TdrStv

COME ON...
LET'S BE FRIENDS :)

We adore our readers and love connecting with them socially.

Like BookSumo on Facebook and let's get social!

Facebook

And also check out the BookSumo Cooking Blog.

Food Lover Blog

Printed in Great Britain
by Amazon